1048·52

1048-56

1048-60

1048-53

1048-57

1048·6?

1048·54

1048-58

1048-62

Alvin Ailey
American Dance Theater

Jack Mitchell Photographs

Alvin Ailey
American Dance Theater

Jack Mitchell Photographs

Foreword by Judith Jamison

Introduction by Richard Philp

A DONNA MARTIN BOOK

Andrews and McMeel | Kansas City

Alvin Ailey American Dance Theater:
Jack Mitchell Photographs
© 1993 by Jack Mitchell
Introduction © 1993 by Richard Philp
Printed in Hong Kong
by Everbest Printing Company, Ltd.
For information write
Andrews and McMeel,
a Universal Press Syndicate Company,
4900 Main Street, Kansas City,
Missouri 64112.

Library of Congress
Cataloging-in-Publication Data

Mitchell, Jack.
Alvin Ailey American Dance Theater / Jack Mitchell,
photographs ; foreword by Judith Jamison ;
introduction by Richard Philp.
p.   cm.
"A Donna Martin book."
ISBN 0-8362-4509-1
1. Alvin Ailey American Dance
Theater—Pictorial works. I. Title.
GV1786.A42M58   1993
792.8′4—dc20
93-13582
CIP

Book Design by
Edward D. King

Foreword

Dancers are fascinated by photographs of their own performances. They confirm the impressions offered by constant, albeit fleeting, glances in the studio mirror. At best, they preserve forever the ephemeral moment when one's body conforms to the movement and something magical happens.

Choreographers also approach photographs of their work with more than passing interest. Questions of proper technique or execution hold second place to insecurities concerning the impact of the work.

It is no surprise, therefore, that "photo sessions" are times of high expectation and anxiety for all concerned.

How fortunate, therefore, that the Alvin Ailey American Dance Theater has had the luxury of working with, and trusting, one photographer, Jack Mitchell, for over thirty years.

Photo sessions with Jack are not tense events, but neither are they the breezy affairs depicted in too many movies. Hard work is engaged in by all concerned. Hard, *creative* work. Choreographers search for the moment which best exemplifies the spirit of the piece. Dancers struggle to repeat lifts and jumps ever higher and more dynamic. Through it all, Jack remains calm, composed, yet demanding and in control. He is no mere chronicler, but an active participant.

For in Jack Mitchell, Alvin found what he looked for so often in his career: a true collaborator. Jack's photographs are not simply reproductions of choreography; they represent a fusion of choreographic and photographic techniques yielding art works of enduring value. Jack's photographs convey the sense of theater that is so basic to the Ailey repertory. Not just a beautiful arabesque or a dynamic leap (although both of these are present in abundance), Jack's images communicate the movement and the drama in the work. A difficult task in a static art form.

Working consistently and successfully with one photographer over such a long period of time has yielded a treasure trove of images. Indeed, the Ailey company is perhaps the best documented of any modern dance company.

Jack's collaboration with the company began just after the creation of two pillars of our repertory: "Blues Suite" and "Revelations." These master works are all the more amazing for the humble situation of the artists who created and performed them. Jack captures beautifully this contrast of big performances on very small budgets.

Fortunately, the collaboration continues; also represented here are the wonderful dancers I work with today. They are creating dance history of their own.

This volume depicts the rapid growth of the company as tour after tour exposed the entire world to Alvin's vision. As dancer replaces dancer, and the now familiar repertory of the company is built, the passion for which the Ailey company is renowned remains.

This is not to say that individual dancers have not left indelible marks on the company. Jack's photographs pay well-deserved homage to many of the world's best dance artists from Jimmy Truitte to Carmen DeLavallade to Dudley Williams to Donna Wood to Gary DeLoatch. And, of course, Alvin, whose talent, warmth, and spirit guided the company from its humble beginnings to its current status as the world's largest modern dance organization. What a pleasure it is to once again see Alvin dancing!

Judith Jamison
Artistic Director,
Alvin Ailey American Dance Theater

Introduction

by Richard Philp

Jack Mitchell is that rarest of all postwar artists, our preeminent photographer of dance. And Alvin Ailey is known worldwide as a dynamic choreographer, champion of contemporary dance, and forceful company director—an artist of the first order who helped define an evolving American art form. The union of these two artistic visions—Mitchell's and Ailey's—is the subject of this exciting new volume, which traces Ailey's remarkable achievement over three decades through Mitchell's lens. In dance, no other collaboration exists like it, no series of photographs that traces a company's progression through the decades or explores the work of a single choreographer over such a sustained, fertile period of popular and artistic achievement. And, frankly, given the fragile nature of the ecostructure of the arts today, it seems unlikely that a photographer of Mitchell's stature will ever have an opportunity to create this kind of project again.

Like Alvin Ailey, the Florida-born (1925) Mitchell grew up in the deep South. His father, an electrician for the Florida East Coast Railroad, taught his son the rudiments of camera work and developing. Some kids are "called" early in life; the much-talked-about conversion experience can happen in the arts just as intensely as it does in religion. Young Jack pursued his muse with a quiet determination from the time he was in his early teens, but it was an encounter with Ted Shawn, perhaps the greatest American male dancer in the first half of the twentieth century, that set the young photographer on his professional course. A few years later, Shawn would also play an important role in Alvin Ailey's shifting from the West Coast to the East; very few men and women in dance in those days were not affected in some way by Shawn. Mitchell and Ailey would not meet, however, until the late 1950s, and their long-standing professional relationship was cemented in 1961. At that time, Mitchell's medium-format photography of American Ballet Theatre dancers was on display during the American Ballet Theatre season and Ailey, who "went to absolutely everything in New York," admired the quality of the photos and wanted Mitchell for himself. Ailey invited Mitchell over to a tiny performing space on Eighth Avenue called the Clark Center and, with his dancers, performed for Mitchell's camera. That was November 1961, and prints from that early shoot are included in this volume. Mitchell's collaboration with the company has continued to this day.

A good photographer is involved with his subject; the genius can actually enhance the images he is creating. Very little, in the hands of a master, happens by accident. An example of the care and feeding a good photographer provides is illustrated by the white umbrella story—this particular umbrella becoming one of the images most closely connected with the irresistible openness and rhapsodic joy of Ailey's greatest single dancework, "Revelations."

Mitchell was among the first photographers to use the underside of a white umbrella as an electronic flash reflector (the result is a softer light with a more diffused quality). But white umbrellas of sufficient substance and texture were generally not available in the early 1960s. (In those days umbrellas were not the fashion statements they have become today, and the plain black variety was the standard.) So Mitchell went to Uncle Sam's Umbrella Shop on West 57th Street in his hometown Manhattan and had one made specifically for his studio work. Ailey was so impressed with the look and feel of the white umbrella—forget about the pictures—that he commandeered the magnificent object and substituted it, forever hence, for the original black bumbershoot he had been using in "Revelations." Chances are, if you know anything about American contemporary dance, you know Mitchell's white reflecting umbrella, even if you've never seen Ailey's ballet "Revelations."

By the 1960s, Mitchell's dance photography became the standard against which other photographers had to gauge their work. His work was being used in publications too numerous to list here, but any list would eventually have to include my own (*Dance Magazine,* for which Mitchell has created over 150 covers) and the *New York Times,* for which he did theater and music, as well as dance. The major photographic images of an entire generation of performing artists were being taken by Mitchell, a fact not lost on Ailey.

Things are never as well organized in fact as they may be in theory, and the creation of a new ballet around the Ailey studios—wherever they happened to be at the time—was no exception. Talking about the creative process, Ailey told me that he often began a new dance with "certain images, visual images that may occur in the dance, of groups of people, of patterns." He talked in photographic terms of "moving stills" and discussed blending, as in action photography, of "several images that, in my mind, eventually become the dance." But it was often an arduous journey from those initial stirrings to the opening night, and a new Ailey dance might still be in process up to the very evening of the first performance. But Ailey knew and trusted his dancers and sometimes relied heavily on their distinctive personalities to carry them over any rough terrain in new works.

On one such occasion in the 1960s, due to the company's touring schedule and the Sunday newspaper's early deadlines, Ailey's newest ballet, as yet untitled, had to be photographed before its completion, long before its completion. Mitchell was told over the phone by Ailey which dancers were going to be used and, beyond that, the rest was left up to Mitchell. The quality of Mitchell's "choreography" for camera was so pleasing that Ailey would come to entrust his new works to the eye of Mitchell's camera on numerous occasions during the years, and those Ailey/Mitchell "works" are well represented in this volume.

Dance is an impermanent art, recorded in the muscle memory of dancers and, if you are fortunate, on film and, more recently, videotape. This volume of photographs—in addition to being a collection of images of magnificent bodies—is also rich in historical connotations, the liveliest kind of permanent record of the works of important creators and creations that formed the nucleus of Ailey's remarkable vision of American dance and what it could be. You will find on these pages the collective essence—the core, the gist, the heart—of what we know today as Ailey dance, which has given so much pleasure around the world.

Ailey often said that we couldn't possibly know where we're going if we don't know where we've already been—as applicable to society as to dancing—and he routinely applied this belief to his own young dancers whom he forever nattered at about the richness of their dance heritage. Alvin Ailey was a strong believer in the good, which he seemed to feel would find a way out, no matter how hard we tried to box it in. His young students, in the school he founded that thrives in the Lincoln Center area of New York City, would have to know "the works of Katherine Dunham, Pearl Primus, or Lester Horton, or José Limón, John Butler, Jimmy Truitte, Anna Sokolow, or Hanya Holm," among many, his list of "musts" being long and abundant and colorful and containing numerous dance works which, unfortunately, with the passage of time, have now been reduced to a sentence or two in the history books.

Half-joking, Ailey often expressed his frustrations at having to choreograph new dances—as many as six in one New York season during the 1970s—when there were so many old "masterpieces" out there by other choreographers waiting for revival. But his adoring public was insatiably hungry for new works, money was always scarce, and his company's board of directors—the source of Ailey's money—wisely kept its collective eye on the box office receipts. New works by Ailey always produced results; his beloved revivals had to wait. But not always: The Dunham retrospective brought the "great lady," as Ailey called her, back into the public eye for a full season; and his revivals of Ted Shawn (the man who helped both Mitchell and Ailey as youngsters), Doris Humphrey, José Limón, and many others introduced new audiences to the glories of historical American modern dance.

Overall, Ailey's accomplishment is enormous and was achieved—and maintained—against all odds. During four decades he choreographed about eighty ballets, creating a body of dance works that have become classics in their genre. But he also created opportunities for other choreographers and dancers whose careers he nurtured and sustained by providing dancers, a stage, and the freedom to create whatever the spirit desired.

"I never wanted to produce whole evenings of just Alvin Ailey," Ailey told me in 1977. "I have always thought that it is much more interesting to see many ideas on a dance program, rather than just one person's ideas. The eclectic element is important, and if more people adopted that position, dance would be better served." Ailey's was a large and generous nature. He was a man who loved to laugh and have a good time and be with his many friends. On countless occasions he proved to be a loyal friend to many artists whose talents might have otherwise been lost to the American stage. And the profits from the good will that Ailey generated in his lifetime continue to pour back into the company, enriching its atmosphere and lightening the load for Ailey's gifted successor, Judith Jamison—the only person, in fact, who could have followed so successfully in Ailey's footsteps.

The Ailey story cuts across the worlds of art and politics and emerges a clear victory for the human spirit. It is a story about wisdom and endurance and depth of feeling—the very substance of Ailey's own often luminous dance works; the very substance, in fact, of the photographs we find in this volume.

Born in 1931 in Rogers, Texas, Ailey grew up in what he called a "closed society," a tight black community in which religion and strong family ties played paramount roles.

"I was a kid during the Depression and my people were farmers. That meant there wasn't much opportunity." In later years, when Ailey reminisced, he tended to portray his growing up in somewhat idyllic terms, and living in rural poverty became "a romantic childhood in which I didn't know about things like lynchings and the Ku Klux Klan. But there was a great, beautiful kind of folk life, with Saturday night cafés and folk singers."

The pungent images of that folk culture would later become the subject matter of Ailey's signature dance works, "Blues Suite" and "Revelations." "I wanted to portray the black community in two ways: the secular and the religious communities. 'Blues' represented things that are very funky and human, fighting and drinking and laughing and great *joie de vivre,* which black people have in the midst of their pain; and the world of 'Revelations' was very religious and dignified."

These contrasting themes, the earthy secular in opposition to the noble religious, were played out in many of his dance roles. Although Ailey was occasionally criticized for the simplicity he resorted to in portraying contrasting characters, particularly his women—the saint and the sinner, the virgin and the whore—he defended himself by reminding us he was a man of the theater, where things had to be simple, clear, easy to understand at a glance. He used what he knew firsthand, what he himself had experienced as a black man living in America in the middle of the twentieth century.

At the age of twelve Ailey moved with his family "from a country ghetto to an urban ghetto," Los Angeles. The Second World War was a boom time and the impressionable youngster with a bent for languages (at one time he seemed headed for a career in academe) came into contact with some "powerful forces—all those forties musicians, films, and dancers." An early, almost chance exposure to the Ballet Russe de Monte Carlo, on tour in L.A. led to his studying modern dance with Lester Horton, who turned out to be the great seminal influence on the young artist's development. "Lester did things that were ethnic, as well as modern; he developed jazz steps and isolations of the hip and torso in a sort of Afro-Asian way." And a few years later, he encountered Jack Cole, another serious influence who had "a kind of masculinity, verve, stylization, and energy that encapsulated for me the tension of the forties and fifties; Jack Cole created the best male dances that I have ever seen—fantastic, brilliant. Nobody makes dances like that anymore."

It was under Horton's influence that Ailey began to choreograph. Tentative, insecure, and by his own admission not very good as a dancer, the young Ailey found in the older Horton a source of much knowledge, wisdom, and encouragement.

After Horton's untimely death in the early 1950s, Ailey came East, first to Ted Shawn's summer festival at Jacob's Pillow, and then on to New York City, where he found work over the next few years dancing in musicals and on the concert stage, performing in a genre that grew out of nightclubs and show business and the film-conscious West Coast. With Donald McKayle, Louis Johnson, and Talley Beatty—dancer/choreographers with whom he worked for many years—Ailey defined the black male concert dancer. In those early years, Ailey legitimized dancing as a career for black men—not a small accomplishment for that era in America when both blacks and dance were very far removed from mainstream concerns. Ailey was as much at home in the musical theater as he was in modern dance, but he soon emerged as a notably better choreographer than many of his contemporaries. They were all struggling, but Alvin was finding his voice; he knew how to shape dance into a theater event.

From the start, he wanted very much to show the "black experience" in his dances, and this became a dominant theme throughout his career. On the West Coast, Lester Horton's company exemplified the kind of energy that could be generated in a multiracial company consisting of blacks, Indians, Mexicans, Asians, and whites. "Lester was trying to do what I have always tried to do, erase the idea of color," he said in 1988. "I always thought the company should be integrated, but when I first came to New York in the 1950s, I didn't know any white dancers. In those days, the black dancers were very close, like a family, and they provided me with the support I needed. I had to learn, so they were the ones who taught me. My company finally became interracial in 1962, which had been my dream all along."

Getting enough money for concerts was always a problem. Following the now-famous "first" concert for twelve dancers on March 30, 1958, at the East Side YM-YWHA (an early center for modern dance), the dancers encountered a fate that was all too common: They had to disband. There was no money. "We'd work six weeks or eight weeks on one concert," Ailey told me, "do one performance, pay everybody ten or fifteen dollars—if I could afford to pay them that much—then after all those weeks of rehearsal without pay, we'd go back to earning a living, such as it was, working at Macy's or Bloomingdale's."

But Ailey's company succeeded because of his genius and persistence and a certain humorous charm that made the tough times easier to take. By the late 1970s, Ailey's persistence would be rewarded with a thriving school—an educational center committed to teaching the diverse techniques that go into making an Ailey dancer—as well as the existence of three companies (the main company and two smaller companies connected with the school). Often ready with a quip, Ailey estimated his success much more simply: "In order to succeed, you only have to do two things: One, get the audiences into the theater. And, two, keep them awake." The packed houses and the cheering, stomping crowds at Ailey performances over many years corroborate his success on his own terms.

"I was not very good as a dancer," Ailey said, "I was more style, like Jack Cole and Lester. I did lots of turns and knee slides and jumps and fell over and rolled on the floor and grabbed the girls and ran across the stage—that kind of thing. I stopped in 1965 when I was thirty-two [sic]."

At first, Ailey's own style of dancing determined the choreography he set and the kind of dancers he selected. "In the first company I was very strong on character dancers, great actors, mimes, personalities. I can't say that they were great dancers; I looked at them for different things; I wanted a theatrical person."

As Ailey's repertoire began to change, he expanded his expectations. "I began to acquire works by Talley Beatty and Jimmy Truitte, we had Carmen de Lavallade and Dudley Williams, who had danced with Graham and Ze'Eva Cohen. Things changed." Dancers such as Clive Thompson were coming from the Graham company, and Ailey acquired works by choreographers such as Limón, Butler, Donald Byrd, Ulysses Dove, Katherine Dunham, Donald McKayle, Billy Wilson, and many others—more than fifty choreographers creating more than 150 works.

Eventually, Ailey's dancers would have to have, as he described it to me, a "good knowledge of Cecchetti and Russian technique, with good placement and sense of line, good carriage, and good feet." But this is a modern company and firm command of Graham and Horton techniques is also essential. In fact, Ailey often described the advantages of American training and American dancers in terms of his own: "The American dancer is very athletic. We're a sports-minded country, and American dancers are more muscular and better built than others; they also have a lot of energy. They are also very competitive. They don't have long careers—five, ten, or fifteen years—and then it's over. But what glorious careers!"

"No other company around today," Ailey told me shortly before his death, "does what we do, requires the same range, challenges both the dancers and the audience to the same intense degree." And he was right. By the time he died on December 1, 1989, Ailey's company had become, in his words, "a unique kind of American dance." And that—the range, the style, the talent, the enormous heart—is what comes across in these pages.

Richard Philp is the editor-in-chief of *Dance Magazine.*

Alvin Ailey
American Dance Theater

Jack Mitchell Photographs

Alvin Ailey dances his "Hermit Songs"on the stage of New York's Clark Center

1961

Alvin Ailey dancing "Hermit Songs"

1961

Alvin Ailey dancing "Hermit Songs"

Bruce Langhorne, Alvin Ailey, Carmen de Lavallade, and
Brother John Sellers in Ailey's "Roots of the Blues"

Alvin Ailey performing his "Roots of the Blues" with Carmen de Lavallade,
Brother John Sellers, and guitarist Bruce Langhorne

Carmen de Lavallade and Alvin Ailey in "Roots of the Blues"

Alvin Ailey and Carmen de Lavallade in "Roots of the Blues"

Carmen de Lavallade dancing John Butler's "The Letter"

Carmen de Lavallade in "The Letter"

Carmen de Lavallade in "The Letter"

1961

Carmen de Lavallade and James Truitte in Lester Horton's "The Beloved"

Alvin Ailey's "Revelations"

1961

Alvin Ailey, Myrna White, James Truitte, Ella Thompson Moore, Minnie
Marshall, and Don Martin in "Revelations"

1961

Minnie Marshall and James
Truitte in "Revelations"

Alvin Ailey, Ella Thompson Moore, and Myrna White in "Revelations"

1961

Myrna White,
Minnie Marshall,
and Ella Thompson Moore
in "Revelations"

Alvin Ailey, Myrna White,
James Truitte, Minnie
Marshall, Don Martin,
and Ella Thompson
Moore in "Revelations"

16

Minnie Marshall, Ella Thompson Moore, and James Truitte in "Revelations"

1962

Alvin Ailey

1962

Alvin Ailey

1964

Takako Asakawa, Hope Clarke, Lucinda Ransom, Joan Peters, and (seated) Loretta Abbott in "Revelations"

1964

Dancers Loretta Abbott, Joan Peters, and Takako Asakawa improvising for the camera

Loretta Abbott in Ailey's "Blues Suite"

Alvin Ailey rehearses Joan Peters in his "Blues Suite" as Loretta Abbott, Kelvin Rotardier, and William Louther watch

Loretta Abbott in Ailey's "Blues Suite"

1964

Hope Clarke in "Blues Suite"

Dudley Williams and Lucinda
Ransom in "Blues Suite"

Lucinda Ransom in "Blues Suite"

Joyce Trisler in a movement from James Truitte's "Variegations," a solo reflecting
the dance technique of Lester Horton

Joyce Trisler and James Truitte in
Lester Horton's "The Beloved"

Joyce Trisler in "Variegations"

1964

William Louther in "Revelations"

Dudley Williams

Miguel Godreau in costume for Talley
Beatty's "The Road of the Phoebe Snow"

1966

Takako Asakawa

1966

Miguel Godreau dancing Sinner Man in Ailey's "Revelations"

30

Miguel Godreau in Geoffrey
Holder's "Prodigal Prince"

1967

Judith Jamison and Miguel Godreau
in "Prodigal Prince"

31

1967

Judith Jamison dancing Geoffrey Holder's "Prodigal Prince"

1967

Miguel Godreau as the "Prodigal Prince"

James Truitte in "Prodigal Prince"

1967

34

Kelvin Rotardier performing "Prodigal Prince," a ballet with choreography,
costume design, and music by Geoffrey Holder

1967

Judith Jamison in Alvin Ailey's "Revelations"

Kelvin Rotardier in "Revelations"

Judith Jamison in "Revelations"

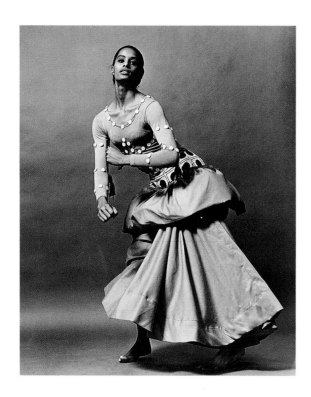

Consuelo Atlas in "Prodigal Prince"

1969

Judith Jamison in Lucas Hoving's "Icarus." Costume design is by Beni Montresor

Dudley Williams in Talley Beatty's
"The Road of the Phoebe Snow"

George Faison in Talley Beatty's
"The Road of the Phoebe Snow"

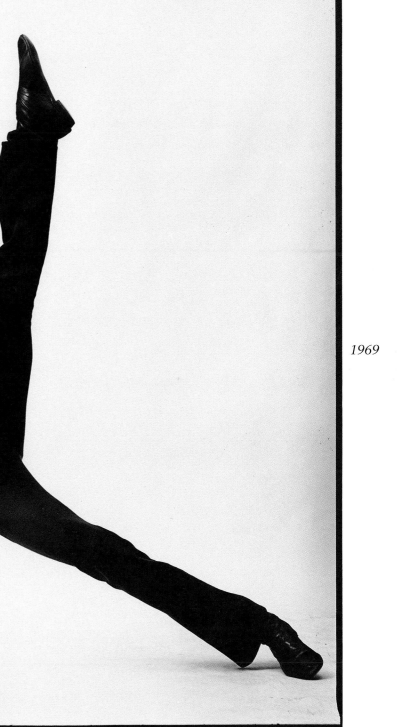

Dudley Williams in "The Road of the Phoebe Snow"

Kelvin Rotardier,
Dudley Williams,
and Judith Jamison
in Talley Beatty's
"Black Belt"

1969

Alma Woolsey,
Danny Strayhorn,
and Sylvia Waters
in Talley Beatty's
"The Road of the
Phoebe Snow"

42

Alma Woolsey in "Quintet"
by Alvin Ailey

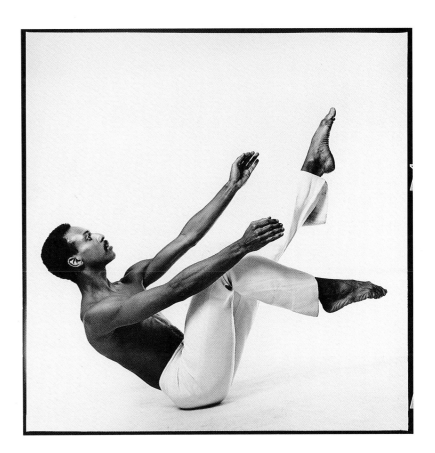

Dudley Williams in Alvin
Ailey's "Revelations"

1969

Renee Rose, Linda Kent, Michelle Murray, Alma Woolsey, and Sylvia Waters in Alvin Ailey's "Quintet"

Ernest Pagnano, Judith Jamison, and George Faison in Talley Beatty's "Congo Tango Palace"

1969

Linda Kent and Dudley Williams in "The Road of the Phoebe Snow"

46

1969

Danny Strayhorn and Renee Rose in Talley Beatty's "The Road of the Phoebe Snow"

1969

Kelvin Rotardier in Talley Beatty's "Congo Tango Palace"

John Parks and Sara Yarborough in Alvin Ailey's "Mary Lou's Mass"

Judith Jamison in "Cry," a solo dance created for her by Alvin Ailey

1971

Judith Jamison in "Cry"

51

1971

Judith Jamison in "Cry"

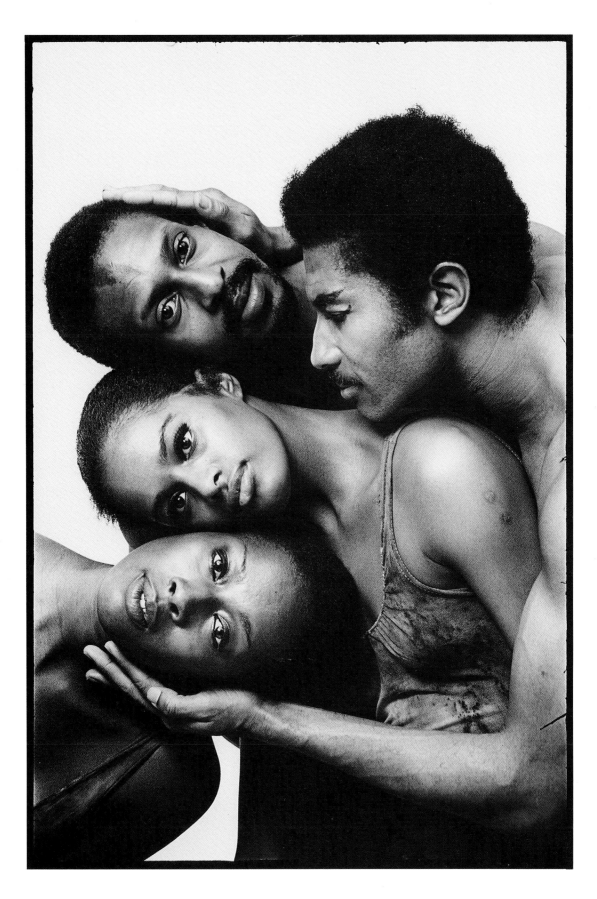

1971

Kelvin Rotardier embracing Judith Jamison, Consuelo Atlas, and Dudley Williams
in Alvin Ailey's "Archipelago"

1971

Dudley Williams, guest artist Lynn Seymour, Ramon Segarra, and Kelvin Rotardier in Alvin Ailey's "Flowers"

Judith Jamison, Clive Thompson, and Kelvin
Rotardier in Alvin Ailey's "Mary Lou's Mass"

Dudley Williams, Kenneth Pearl, and Sara Yarborough
in Donald McKayle's "Rainbow 'Round My Shoulder"

Sara Yarborough and Judith Jamison in John Butler's "Carmina Burana"

Sara Yarborough, Freddy
Romero, and John Parkes,
at top, improvising for
the camera

1973

Sara Yarborough, John
Parkes, Michihiko Oka,
and Judith Jamison
in a moment from John
Butler's "Carmina Burana"

1975

Judith Jamison and Sarita Allen in
Alvin Ailey's "The Mooche"

Sarita Allen in "The Mooche"

Alvin Ailey and Judith Jamison pose after the "Carmina Burana"–"The Mooche" photo call

1976 Judith Jamison dancing John Butler's "Facets"

Dudley Williams in George Faison's
"Hobo Sapiens"

Judith Jamison dancing John Butler's "Facets"

1976

Dudley Williams, Elbert Watson, and Clive Thompson in Alvin Ailey's "Three Black Kings"

1977

Donna Wood in Louis
Falco's "Caravan"

Estelle Spurlock in
Alvin Ailey's "Cry"

1977

Estelle Spurlock in Alvin Ailey's "The Lark Ascending"

Donna Wood in George Faison's "Gazella"

Judith Jamison (center), surrounded by Donna Wood, Sarita Allen, Estelle Spurlock, Mari Kajiwara,
Jody Moccia, and Melvin Jones in Alvin Ailey's "Revelations"

1978

Alvin Ailey (center), surrounded by dancers on stage at New York's City Center during the twentieth-anniversary season of the Alvin Ailey American Dance Theater: Charles Adams, Sarita Allen, Marilyn Banks, Alistair Butler, Masazumi Chaya, Ulysses Dove, Ronni Favors, Nicky Harrison, Judith Jamison, Melvin Jones, Mari Kajiwara, Keith McDaniel, Jody Moccia, Steven Mones, Milton Myers, Michihiko Oka, Carl Paris, Maxine Sherman, Beth Shorter, Estelle Spurlock, Clive Thompson, Dudley Williams, Donna Wood, Peter Woodin, and Rehearsal Director Mary Barnett

1979

Gary DeLoatch, Donna Wood, and Alistair Butler rehearse Alvin Ailey's "Memoria"

Alvin Ailey

Gary DeLoatch, Donna Wood, and Alistair Butler rehearse Alvin Ailey's "Memoria"

1979

Michihiko Oka improvising for the camera

70

Sara Yarborough and Carl
Bailey in Billy Wilson's
"Concerto in F"

Keith McDaniel, Maxine Sherman,
and April Berry rehearse Choo
San Goh's "Spectrum"

Mari Kajiwara and Keith McDaniel (in front), with Maxine Sherman, Kevin Brown,
and Gary DeLoatch rehearse Alvin Ailey's "Satyriade"

Gary DeLoatch in Alvin Ailey's "Satyriade"

Keith McDaniel, Kevin Brown, and Mari Kajiwara in Alvin Ailey's "Satyriade"

Maxine Sherman in Alvin
Ailey's "Landscape"

1982

Sarita Allen in Elisa
Monte's "Pigs and Fishes"

Maxine Sherman in Alvin Ailey's "Landscape"

1982

Sarita Allen in Elisa Monte's "Pigs and Fishes"

1983

Rodney Nugent, Ronald Brown,
Kevin Brown, Keith McDaniel,
Danny Clark, and Gregory Stewart
in Bill T. Jones's "Fever Swamp"

Gary DeLoatch, Donna Wood,
Keith McDaniel, and Sharrell Mesh
in John Butler's "Seven Journeys"

Judith Jamison (front) choreographing her "Divining" with Masazumi Chaya and Donna Wood

Ralph Glenmore (in air), and
Masazumi Chaya in Jennifer
Mueller's "Speeds"

Marilyn Banks, Neisha Folkes, Renee Robinson, and Deborah Manning in
"How to Walk an Elephant" by Bill T. Jones and Arnie Zane

Danny Clark in Louis Johnson's "Lament"

1985

Danny Clark in Louis Johnson's "Lament"

Gary DeLoatch and Marilyn Banks in Alvin Ailey's "Caverna Magica"

Gary DeLoatch in Alvin Ailey's
"For 'Bird'—With Love"

1986

Carl Bailey, Deborah Chase, and Gary DeLoatch in Alvin Ailey's "For 'Bird'—With Love"

1986

Debora Chase, Marilyn Banks, Gary DeLoatch, Dudley Williams, Neisha Folkes,
Barbara Pouncie, and Ralph Glinmore in Alvin Ailey's "For 'Bird'—With Love"

Elizabeth Roxas and Rodney
Nugent in Alvin Ailey's
"The Lark Ascending"

Deborah Manning and David
St. Charles in Alvin Ailey's
"The Lark Ascending"

Elizabeth Roxas in Alvin Ailey's
"The Lark Ascending"

1986

Neisha Folkes
in Alvin Ailey's
"For 'Bird'—
With Love"

Elizabeth Roxas in Alvin Ailey's "The Lark Ascending"

Adrienne Armstrong and
Dudley Williams in Alvin
Ailey's "For 'Bird'—With
Love"

1986

April Berry in Alvin
Ailey's "Caverna Magica"

1987

Rodney Nugent and Gary DeLoatch
in Katherine Dunham's "L'Ag'Ya"

Ruthlyn Salomon, Max
Luna, and Marilyn Banks
in Katherine Dunham's
"Los Indios"

Desiree Vlad, Marilyn Banks, Nasha Thomas, and Renee Robinson in Katherine Dunham's "Afrique"

Max Luna, Dwight Rhoden, and Raymond Harris in Alvin Ailey's "Revelations"

Andre Tyson, Stephen
Smith, and Carl Bailey
in Alvin Ailey's
"Revelations"

1988

Renee Robinson and
Andre Tyson in Alvin
Ailey's "Revelations"

1988

Andre Tyson and Marilyn Banks
in Alvin Ailey's "Blues Suite"

Sharrell Mesh and Andre Tyson in
Alvin Ailey's "Opus Mc Shann"

94

1988

Marilyn Banks in Alvin Ailey's "Blues Suite"

April Berry in Alvin Ailey's
"Opus McShann"

April Berry, Sharrell Mesh,
and Debora Chase in Alvin
Ailey's "Blues Suite"

1988

Adrienne Armstrong in Alvin Ailey's "Blues Suite"

1988

Ruthlyn Salomons and Debora Chase in
Ulysses Dove's "Vespers"

Renee Robinson and Debora Chase in
Ulysses Dove's "Vespers"

1988

Renee Robinson and Andre Tyson in Alvin Ailey's "Blues Suite"

A 1988 portrait of Masazumi Chaya, now associate artistic director of the Alvin Ailey American Dance Theater

Renee Robinson in Alvin Ailey's "Cry"

1988

Marilyn Banks, Dudley Williams, Alvin Ailey, and Gary DeLoatch pose during a photo session break

1988

Carl Bailey and Kevin Brown in Alvin
Ailey's "Opus McShann"

Max Luna, Dwight
Rhoden, Desmond
Richardson, and
Dereque Whiturs
in Donald Byrd's
"Shards"

April Berry and Dana
Hash in Lester Horton's
"Sarong Paramaribo"

1989

Desmond Richardson,
Dereque Whiturs,
Duane Cyrus, and
Gary DeLoatch in
Donald McKayle's
"Rainbow 'Round
My Shoulder"

104

1989

Renee Robinson and Carl Bailey in Donald McKayle's "Rainbow 'Round My Shoulder"

1989   Wesley Johnson III, Renee Robinson, Desmond Richardson, Neisha Folkes, Dwight Rhoden, Debora Chase, Elizabeth Roxas, and Stephen Smith in Ulysses Dove's "Episodes"

The Ailey dancers in Talley Beatty's "Come and Get the Beauty of It Hot"

Carl Bailey, Renee Robinson,
and Gary DeLoatch in Talley
Beatty's "Come and Get
the Beauty of It Hot"

Duane Cyrus, Wesley Johnson III,
Aubrey Lynch II, Gary DeLoatch,
Dereque Whiturs, Carl Bailey, and
Don Bellamy in front of Kevin Brown
and Stephen Smith lifting Elizabeth
Roxas in Talley Beatty's "Come and
Get the Beauty of It Hot"

1989

Elizabeth Roxas and Desmond Richardson in Donald McKayle's "Rainbow 'Round My Shoulder"

Aubrey Lynch II and Nasha Thomas in Barry Martin's "Chelsea's Bells"

Renee Robinson, Dwight Rhoden, Debora Chase, and Desmond Richardson in Ulysses Dove's "Episodes"

1990

Wesley Johnson, Dereque Whiturs, Dwight Rhoden, Aubrey Lynch II, and Tracy Inman in Alvin Ailey's "Hidden Rites"

Deborah Manning in Alvin Ailey's "Cry"

Aubrey Lynch II in Judith Jamison's "Forgotten Time"

David St. Charles in Alvin Ailey's "Hidden Rites"

Karine Plantadit, Dwight Rhoden, and Antonio
Carlos Scott in Donald Byrd's "Dance at the Gym"

Nasha Thomas and Dwight Rhoden in
Alvin Ailey's "Pas de Duke"

1991

Elizabeth Roxas and
Desmond Richardson in
Elisa Monte's "Treading"

Desmond Richardson in Louis Falco's "Escargot"

Aubrey Lynch II in Donald McKayle's "District Storyville"

1991

Don Bellamy, Renee Robinson,
and Nasha Thomas in Alvin
Ailey's "Revelations"

1991

Dwight Rhoden, Desmond Richardson,
and Aubrey Lynch II in Alvin Ailey's
"Revelations"

Sarita Allen and Don Bellamy
in Elisa Monte's "Treading"

117

Aubrey Lynch II, Desmond Richardson, and Andre Tyson perform experimental choreography by Masazumi Chaya

1991

Andre Tyson and Dana Hash perform experimental choreography by Masazumi Chaya

Andre Tyson, Dana Hash, and Aubrey Lynch II perform experimental choreography by Masazumi Chaya

1991

Andre Tyson in Alvin Ailey's solo "Hermit Songs"

Jonathan Riseling improvising for photo session

Debora Chase in
Alvin Ailey's "Cry"

1992

Elizabeth Roxas and Dwight Rhoden in Ulysses Dove's "Episodes"

1992

Leonard Meek in Alvin Ailey's "The River"

Toni Pierce in Jawole Willa Jo Zollar's "Shelter"

Lydia Roberts, Michael Joy, Raquelle
Chavis, and Desiree Vlad in Alvin
Ailey's "Blues Suite"

1992

Danielle Gee, Raquelle Chavis, Deborah Manning, Toni Pierce,
and Desiree Vlad in Jawole Willa Jo Zollar's "Shelter"

1992

Aubrey Lynch II in Louis Johnson's
"Fontessa and Friends"

Desmond Richardson in Louis
Johnson's "Fontessa and Friends"

126

Renee Robinson in Alvin Ailey's "Blues Suite"

1992

Desmond Richardson in Lar Lubovitch's "North Star"

128

1993

Directors and dancers of the Alvin Ailey American Dance Theater at the beginning of the company's thirty-fifth year. *On floor front:* Nasha Thomas, Andre Tyson, Sarita Allen; *second row:* Troy Powell, Desmond Richardson, Renee Robinson, Artistic Director Judith Jamison, Associate Artistic Director Masazumi Chaya, Deborah Manning, Dwight Rhoden; *third row:* Marilyn Banks, Michael Thomas, Dana Hash, Jonathan Phelps, Toni Pierce, Elizabeth Roxas, Aubrey Lynch II; *fourth row:* Tracy Inman, Matthew Rushing, Raquelle Chavis, Michael Joy, Roger Bellamy, Dudley Williams, Desiree Vlad, Duane Cyrus; *top row:* Leonard Meek, Karine Plantadit, Danielle Gee, Linda-Denise Evans, Antonio Carlos Scott, Lydia Roberts